THE LOVE FACTOR

PRAYER CHANGES THINGS

VISIONARY - PROPHETESS

JENNIFER NICHOLS

COMPILED BY HER

Book Cover Design: Dr. Shadaria Allison | Nichol LeAnn Perricci, DNP Designs

Interior Book Design & Formatting: TamikaINK.com

Editor: Dr. Tamika Hall| TamikaINK.com

Published By: Igniting The Flame Publishing

Library of Congress Cataloging-in-Publication Data has been applied for

ISBN: 9798397409025

PRINTED IN THE UNITED STATES OF AMERICA

Endorsement
By Dr. Deborah Allen

The Love Factor "Prayer Changes Things" is an exceptional book that I highly recommend to anyone seeking guidance on improving their lives through prayer. The authors of this inspirational anthology do an excellent job of exploring the power of prayer and how it can transform our circumstances. This book provides readers with a wealth of information and practical tips on how to pray effectively, highlighting the importance of love and faith in the process. I was deeply inspired by the author's personal stories of triumph over adversity through the power of prayer. This book is a powerful reminder that with faith, hope, and love, anything is possible. Whether you are a seasoned believer or just starting on your spiritual journey, The Love Factor "Prayer Changes Things" is a must-read that will uplift, inspire, and empower you to live a life filled with hope, love, and abundance. I want to say congratulations and job well done to the Visionary, Prophetess Jennifer Nichols, and every Co-Author.

Apostle Dr. Deborah Allen
Visionary of Igniting The Flame Publishing
www.ignitingtheflamepublishing.com

Table of Contents

Introduction

This book is dedicated to the Father, Son, and the Holy Spirit as we express our testimonies and gratitude through prayer, the study of His word, and life challenges. We speak of his goodness and mercy toward us and our families in the difficult and in the times of Joy. We give you praise as he has kept his promises to all of us, but it was through our faith, through our obedience, through our intimacy in prayer, study and showing ourselves approved, fasting, and sacrifices of love toward him, and in the same token we give him honor.

We collaborated knowing that our Father is using our stories to encourage, give you tools, and strengthen your faith as you go forward in your own journey. All praise be to him. I want to thank every woman who sacrificed her time, family, and life to write this book. The purpose is to heal, restore, and spread the truth of the word of the Lord through our collaborations and stories that ground us and surround us with the love of Christ, making you aware of the love and intimacy that prayer has given us, and the power and authority it has a forwarded us through our communication with him. It can do the same for you!

Sustained Love
By Jennifer Nichols

You sustained me through pain; you healed me through heartache; you let me be troubled to free me from the rubble. You set me up on high and gave me a brand new life; you delivered me from myself and kept me and protected me when death was trying to devour me. You showed up when no one else with you stayed with me when none could. You directed my reins; you sustained all the same. You strengthened me; when I was drained, you loved me when I was the pain. You kept me solid when I wanted to fall you made me late just to get involved. You showed me what love was; you made me see myself when no one else cared at all. You captured me with your love by giving me all you got and never withdrawing. You brought me from a low place like Joseph; you made space. You elevated me when I was low; you gave me hope when I could not see tomorrow. You gave me a future hope and an expected end. You silenced my enemies until no end. You pushed me further when I didn't want to go high; you made me uncomfortable knowing to say goodbye and set me up for failure to keep needing you.

You give me joy because I'm new. You gave me an inheritance, family, and hope; you gave me your Son, Jesus, whom no one could outvote. You trusted me when I could not trust myself; you said no when you saw something else. You gave me eyes to see and ears to hear; you gave me tears to clear my fears. You made my brain clear when it was unclear. You spoke peace and stillness to my heart. You made my way straight when I wanted to depart.

You cast out demons I never knew were there. You did it like no one that I could compare. You said it's my time, so I take you up on that; you declare your word, and that's a fact. You sense danger and cover me. You see me struggle financially and set me in order of victory. You give me instructions and strategy. You hid my face from vanity; you kept my family.

You, dear God, have sustained me, and Father, I ask that you continue to be my sustaining father, my help, and my love to treasure you from above and to sustain all those who read the victories, testimonies, and prayers we have received. May they receive it as we have many. I give them the knowledge to understand that your love is better than a man's.

May I write my love letter to God that gives me charge to bombard heaven with alarm? May those who read receive be encouraged that the good Lord knows that sometimes you will feel discouraged. But trample the discouragement through these words; you and I are victorious, and be encouraged! May sustaining love continue to be our portion in the natural and the spiritual, for you cause us to avail much by you giving us strength and stamina! It is so that you have bestowed mercy through your sustaining love you captured me and given me joy in the midst of it. 1 Peter 4:8 Above all, keep loving one another earnestly since love covers a multitude of sins."

His sustaining love made me walk away from a life of prostitution, homelessness, and neglect.; Embraced me where I was when I searched for love in all the wrong places I was wanted from every race, color, and creed, but no one wanted my spirit;

they wanted what I obtained naturally for show. Jesus wanted all of me and was the only one who did not abandon me in my ugly moments and my weak days; he kept me.

I sought purity from the point I was tired of my body being used and being alone, and I wanted substance. I would go to hotels with my next boyfriend after he bought me dinner and maybe a movie. It was not God's best. I would walk from the Jewel Osco because I didn't have enough money to pay for the bus fare to be ashamed to ask for help. One night there was a black SUV that pulled up on me as if I was a hooker!

He asked me if I wanted a ride I was smart enough to stay in a populated and lighted area, and I told him no! But I knew I was in danger as he looked to want to grab me, but before he could utter another word, the cops pulled up behind him and asked me what was going on. I told them that I was not a prostitute I was just trying to walk home from work. They asked me if I wanted a ride. I breathed a huge sigh and said yes. They took me home, and I was safe! The moment I got home I went got in my bed and went to sleep.

I started praying for a husband at twenty years old because the world told me it was okay to sleep around and be passed around like a marijuana joint, but in reality, dating in the world is prostitution and unhealthy to the spirit and the mind. It was promoted to be promiscuous and out there in movies and music videos, but you don't get the total picture that you are degraded, disrespected, and disregarded. Not even treated like a human, as a woman! I wanted to get my purity back and keep it!

No one could tell me who I was or wasn't or who I was supposed to be.

Men were like kryptonite in a way for me as over and over again, I had negative encounters of date rape, molestation, abandonment, and many other issues that fed my spirit the wrong thinking toward men. I could not trust them! I grew better in my relationship with my husband as healing while in the marriage, but I also had to overcome it at the same time. It taught me to trust again but also to not lean on men to do what only God can do but only trust in him to heal and restore what is new.

I had to learn to allow him to take care of me I was used to taking care of myself, being that I started working at nine years old working in my grandfather's restaurant making banana pudding with my grandmother and cousins in the summertime in Chicago was the best! He had a restaurant on the south side of Chicago called Trailer Court in which he served soul food, mac and cheese, green beans, gravy chicken, burgers, and many other foods that were on the menu. It was a buffet-style restaurant where people would walk up to look in the protective glass to see what they wanted. There was a basketball hoop in the back of the restaurant where my brother and I played basketball with the co-owners son Ethan.

Those were good memories of my childhood and when I still had some form of innocence in me. Ethan was a bit peculiar, but I liked him as a friend; mostly, my brother stayed at the restaurant while I worked with my grandmother on the dessert at home, cutting bananas, making meringue, and using sweet condensed and evaporated milk for the inside the back before baking the meringue on top of the pudding. My cousins Toya and Yolonda would be a part of the family assembly as we prep and baked and let the pudding rest to take to the restaurant. I remember coming to Chicago in the summertime from Carbondale and then Mississippi and going to the park district with my cousins. It was so fun because I basically had to learn to swim the old fashion way, jump in the pull, and float. It was the same when I came to visit my dad.

Speaking of visiting my dad, it was depressing as he was married to my stepmother at that time and had been divorced from my mother for about eight years. Even though I was mistreated by her, it was even stronger in that I became a better person in how I chose to treat people better than I was treated. I remember the admittance to a mental hospital and told my father that I told her I wanted to be admitted. That was a betrayal that touched not only my life but affected my relationship with my father. I had just turned eighteen years old! I started my adult years in a mental hospital!

In a way, it was a relief getting away from the chaos, but it was what it was deception! The Lord knew all of these things would happen, and he used me to minister to a few kids in the facility, and

I gained and a newfound perspective on life! He is sustaining love in my darkest hour! These stories make up for who I have become today a mixture of the good, the bad, and the ugly.

I lived in a trailer park filled with people running from criminals to single moms. It taught me about life from a young age. Life is like a box of poker cards; you never know what you will be handed, but you play your hand, hope you get an ace or strategize to win! Like Joseph with the coat of many colors when you are in the dungeon, if you trust God as he did, he may raise you up to be In the palace. Pray as Joseph did for wisdom and instruction and wait for the Lord to release to you, then obey, and he will provide.

Read Genesis 37

5 Joseph had a dream, and when he told it to his
brothers, they hated him all the more.
6 He said to them, "Listen to this dream I had: **7**
We were binding sheaves of grain out in the field
when suddenly my sheaf rose and stood upright,
while your sheaves gathered around mine and
bowed down to it."

8 His brothers said to him, "Do you intend to
reign over us? Will you actually rule us?" And they
hated him all the more because of his dream and
what he had said.
9 Then he had another dream, and he told it to
his brothers. "Listen," he said, "I had another
dream, and this time the sun and moon and
eleven stars were bowing down to me."
10 When he told his father as well as his brothers,
his father rebuked him and said, "What is this
dream you had? Will your mother and I and your
brothers actually come and bow down to the
ground before you?" **11** His brothers were jealous
of him, but his father kept the matter in mind.

The blessing of the hard ache can be used for a breakthrough with prayer, and the study of the word as you learn to know the father as I did.

Jennifer Nichols

Jennifer Nichols has in mind Vision build Her is among the yearly call for this tremendous time in her life where she envisions international women and people of every economic and environmental background to flourish with creating through writing and skills draw that out, says Jennifer Nichols, Author of in motion Love Conquers all, the Love factor and The Healing Cloth, the power of healing through prayers, a speaker, ministry leader, and Co-CEO of Clean up and Let's Save, and Let's Birth Your Book and Collena's Corner constructed to help women and youth sell retail products, and write their stories to create wealth through new skills and perfect spreading their message. She has invested in mentorship and coaching, helping her strategize and build wealth. In turn, she is creating the same with her consistent client growth One of her favorite scriptures is Write the vision, makes it plain Habakkuk 2:2!

Jennifer's mandate is this: Her goal is to push women, and youth left behind and broken to heal internally and externally by restoring faith in their lives, leading them back to Christ and a better life! To establish order amongst the saints in the eyes of the creator.

In ministry for fifteen years and thriving, Jennifer is called to set the captives free and bring liberty to the youth and the lost, serving in the children's ministry for three years and prophetic prayer ministry. She is currently a member of

Presence Church in Chicago Heights, Il. Jennifer is Robert Nichols's wife and CEO of Cleanup and Let's Save. She is the mother of three boys, the oldest, Jalen Nichols, middle Jacob Nichols, and the youngest, Jamel Nichols.

To Contact her:
Phone :312-280-5783
To order books,
www.letsbirthyourbook.com

Get my latest ebook, The Love Factor

The Power of Prayer By Dr. Deborah Allen

*Prayer - **a solemn** request for help or expression of thanks addressed to God or an object of worship.*

Prayer is spending intimate time with our Creator, God. I grew up hearing that having little prayer is little power and much prayer is much power. We need to pray because prayer is a powerful and transformative force that has the ability to bring about healing, transformation, and positive change in our lives and the world around us. Through prayer, we can connect with the higher power (God), find solace in times of struggle, and gain the strength and resilience needed to overcome life's challenges. Prayer offers us a sense of purpose, meaning, and connection, reminding us that we are not alone and that there is a greater plan at work in our lives. So, let us embrace the power of prayer and allow it to guide us on our journey toward a more peaceful, loving, and fulfilling life. The power of prayer is a profound and transformative force that has the ability to change lives, circumstances, and even the world. For centuries, people of faith have turned to prayer as a means of seeking guidance, strength, and healing. Whether in times of joy or sorrow, prayer has been a source of comfort and hope, a way to connect with a higher power and find peace amidst the chaos of life.

There are countless stories of the power of prayer, of individuals, churches, and communities coming together in prayer to overcome seemingly insurmountable obstacles. From medical miracles to societal change, prayer has played a pivotal role in bringing about transformation and positive change. According to a 2019 study by the Pew Research Center, about 80% of people worldwide identify with a religious group. Prayer is a common practice within these religious groups, although the frequency and style of prayer can vary widely depending on the individual's beliefs and cultural practices. It is important to note that not all individuals who identify with a religious group may engage in prayer, and there may be some individuals who engage in prayer outside of traditional religious frameworks as well.

One such story is that of a woman named Maria, who was diagnosed with stage 4 cancer. Despite undergoing several rounds of chemotherapy and radiation, her condition continued to deteriorate, and the doctors gave her just a few months to live. Maria, a devout Christian, turned to prayer to find solace and hope in the face of her illness.

She began to pray every day, asking God for healing and strength, and her faith began to grow. She also asked her family and friends to pray for her, and they rallied around her, offering words of encouragement and support.

Over time, Maria's condition began to improve, and her doctors were amazed at her progress. Her tumors began to shrink, and her energy and vitality returned. She continued to pray and trust in God, and eventually, she was declared cancer-free. Maria's story is just one example of the power of prayer in action. It shows that even in the most dire of circumstances, prayer can bring about healing and transformation. It demonstrates that faith and prayer can provide the strength and resilience needed to overcome life's challenges and come out stronger on the other side.

But the power of prayer is not just limited to physical healing. It can also bring about emotional and spiritual healing, helping individuals to find peace, clarity, and purpose in their lives. Prayer can offer a sense of connection and belonging, reminding us that we are not alone and that there is a higher power watching over us. Prayer can also bring about societal change, as seen throughout history with movements such as the civil rights movement and the abolition of slavery. These movements were grounded in faith and prayer, with individuals and communities coming together to pray for justice, equality, and freedom. Through their prayers, they were able to bring about lasting change and transform society for the better.

The power of prayer is not limited to any one religion or belief system. People of all faiths and backgrounds can harness the power of prayer to bring about positive change in their lives and the world around them. It is a universal language that transcends cultural and linguistic barriers, bringing people together in a shared sense of hope and faith.

In conclusion, the power of prayer is a truly remarkable force that has the ability to change things in ways we cannot even begin to imagine. It can bring about physical healing, emotional and spiritual healing, and even societal change. It offers us a sense of comfort, hope, and purpose in a world that can often feel overwhelming and chaotic. So, let us take the time to pray, to connect with a higher power, and to harness the transformative power of prayer to bring about positive change in our lives and the world around us. Be ignited in this season of your life to pray because it is your power of hope and change!

Acknowledgments

For Apostle Dr. Glen Allen Sr, who believed in & saw the fierceness in me!

Written also to acknowledge that the love we have for Jesus always draws us to speak and communicate with him. Also written for everyone that has felt like they could never get back up. It is possible not only to get up but get up, go after what you really want, and win.

"When walking in purpose, fiercely walk in divine authority!"

Apostle Dr. Deborah Allen

Dr. Deborah Allen

Finding one's *inner voice*, can be a liberating, awe-inspiring, and transformational experience. Fashioned to help the masses find their "fierce"; is the dynamic professional, Deborah Allen.

Deborah Allen is a 34X best-selling & 17X international best-selling author, speaker, certified life-coach, cleric, and CEO and creative founder of **The Fierce System**; a multifaceted liaison specialty, centered around helping women to both, find and develop, their voice. Having been trained by world-renowned NSA motivational speaker, Mr. Les Brown, Deborah understands the importance of strategy, development, and credible mentorship; traits she seamlessly translates, to her growing clientele.

Deborah's mantra is simple: Her one and only goal is to motivate clients; helping them to create the life, they were meant to live.

Refusing mediocrity on all fronts, Deborah has trailblazed a credible path for those she serves. She has served as Senior Pastor of Lighthouse Apostolic Ministries of God Church, for the last 23 years; and is the Executive Director of the nonprofit organization, L.A.M. Ministries, Inc.

Matching servant leadership with an incredible respect for higher learning, Deborah is a Certified Life Coach; and is a member of the

National Speaker Association Speaker (NSA) and a Black Speakers Network (BSN) Speaker. Her conglomerate The Fierce System, is comprised of many platforms, including: Fierce TV, Radio, and blog; as well as Fierce Voices of Destiny Program; where she mentors, develops, and creates strategic alignment between clients, and their true life's calling. She is the Visionary and CEO of Igniting The Flame Publishing, Visionary Coaching & Consulting Group LLC and Deborah Allen Enterprise.

Deborah proudly attests that women are at the heartbeat of all she does, and that it is her desire to see them be strong, fierce, and know, that they can truly achieve their dreams, and walk in purpose. When she is not out helping women to come alive, rebuild, shift and find themselves again; Deborah is a valued asset to her communal body, and a loving member of her family and friendship circles.

Dr. Deborah Allen. Energizer. Organizer. Servant Leader.

Apostle Dr. Deborah Allen ~ Contact Information

Igniting The Flame Publishing:
https://www.ignitingtheflamepublishing.com
Links:
Facebook: https://www.facebook.com/deborahallenfierce
Instagram: https://www.instagram.com/deborahallenfierce/
Twitter: https://twitter.com/deborahallenfie
Periscope: https://www.pscp.tv/ladydeborahallen/follow
LinkedIn: https://www.linkedin.com/in/prophetessdeborahallen/
YouTube: https://www.youtube.com/channel/UCTOf0igcAxlVaneH2ZOo_Zg
1st Website: https://deborahallenfierce.com/

2nd Website: https://deborahallenspeaker.com/

The Fierce, Ignition & Activation Show/Podcast:
https://envisionedbroadcasting.com/fierceignition%26activation?fbclid=IwAR03g_k7RO44QE1Ybahy2poVzktBDv08wX07e1X4N0yPF0Spi_MEataMG-o
Email: deborahallenfierce@gmail.com

Weird Girl
By Beatrice White

I loved going to school. I liked learning new things. However, middle school was hard for me. It seemed that I just didn't "fit" in with everyone else. I had a few friends, but no one that I was close to. I remember it like it was yesterday. I was sitting in History class, desperately trying to focus on what Mr. Shoaf was discussing. It was a struggle because he had a very monotone voice that could easily put you to sleep. I was determined to pay attention because we had an upcoming test, and I wanted to get a good grade. I looked around me. The white concrete walls were trying to contain a classroom full of 8th graders who couldn't wait for class to be over. The black chalkboard contained information that most of us would never use again but had to learn.

Mr. Shoaf was a little short man with red hair and a thick red mustache. He was trying his best to make history class as exciting as possible. I noticed some of my classmates were sleeping. Some were nodding off, but very few were paying attention. I was sitting close to the back, where I preferred to sit in all my classes if I had a choice. Sitting in front of me were two of my friends. They were trying to whisper to each other, but unfortunately for me; I was able to hear their conversation in the midst of other conversations that other students were trying to have quietly instead of paying attention to Mr. Shoaf.

I heard one girl say, "She needs to do something with her messed up hair.

Then the other girl said. "Somebody needs to take her shopping; those clothes are so old looking. Beatrice is weird, but she's not a bad person."

I sat back and looked down at my clothes. I was wearing an orange striped long-sleeve shirt that was neatly tucked in and a pair of black jeans that were a little too faded, and a pair of imitation Keds shoes. I felt so embarrassed at what I had on. I looked at my hair. It was short, but my aunt gave me a braid on each side. I thought it was cute, and I had a small bang. My grandmother didn't have the money to take me to the salon, so she did the best she could with my hair. I would often ask her if I could go to the salon to get my hair done, and the answer was always "no" and that she didn't have the money for that. I sat there as if I didn't hear them. I sat there, wishing the bell would ring so I could get out of there. Then one of the girls said she was "weird, what black person listens to classical and rock music."

The other girl trying to whisper, responded, "All she does is read books and all that stuff that nerds do." Then they both chuckled.

"She needs different glasses too," was said.

This was one of the times I wished I had gone to sleep in class. I felt horrible. I have been wearing glasses since I was eight years old. I was nearsighted and had astigmatism, which made me have thick lenses. Since my lenses were thick, I didn't have too many choices when it came to frames. My frames were brown and square-shaped. They were not very flattering, but my choices were even more limited since I had Medicaid. These were the only frames I kind of liked. I sat there feeling so embarrassed and ugly. That was one of those moments that if I could have disappeared, I would have. When I heard these things coming from my "friends," it really hurt.

I began to question myself. Am I that different from everyone else? Is there anything wrong with being black and liking classical and rock music? As I sat in history class, the biggest question I asked myself was, "Why do I have to be me? Why can't I be someone else?

Psalms 139:14
I will praise thee; for I am fearfully and wonderfully made: marvelous are thy works; and that my soul knoweth right well.

God tells us that we should not have to question who we are. He created us in His image. He tells us that because He made us, we are marvelous. The word marvelous means: causing wonder or astonishment, having the characteristics of a miracle of the highest kind or quality. I love this scripture because it says that my soul knows. My soul, which is my mind, will, and intellect, knows that I'm marvelous because I'm created in the image of God! I struggled for years with accepting myself for who I am. It was hard for me to accept that this scripture was talking about me. It was telling me who I am in Christ. It amazed me that I professed that the bible was true, yet this scripture was hard for me to accept that it pertained to me also. I thank the Holy Spirit for showing me that I am loved, wanted, and accepted because I am a child of God.

When I think back on the middle school incident, it has caused me to be more accepting of people regardless of how they look. I am more drawn to the "social outcasts" because I have experienced feeling like an outcast. I try to love people and help them see that they are loved, needed, and accepted and have something to offer this world. Pray this prayer with me.

Father God, I pray that every person that struggles to see themselves as fearfully and wonderfully made that you open their eyes to see who they are in you. Father, I pray you pour out an abundance of love. I pray that you touch the hearts that are feeling unloved, unwanted, and rejected and that they will experience your love, and your acceptance. I pray that we will also show love to those we come in contact with. I pray that peace will be with us because we are secure in who You created us to be.

Amen

Beatrice White

Beatrice is passionate about empowering women and young girls to live a life of purpose and destiny. She is a trauma survivor and is dedicated to helping others overcome trauma and live a victorious life. She is a licensed and ordained minister. She serves faithfully at BSM Throne of His Glory Ministry. She serves as the personal assistant to her pastor. She also teaches bible studies and serves where she is needed. Beatrice has a degree in Theology and Psychology. She is also a Certified Mental Health Coach. She is passionate about working with individuals with mental health concerns. Beatrice is also part of Aglow International, serving as Workplace President. She is involved in street ministry and serving at the shelter. She is a loving wife and mother.

Praying Through
By Alicia Siryon-Wells

Rejoice in our confident hope.
Be patient in trouble,
and keep on praying.
Romans 12:12

Life's challenges can come through varying circumstances, through different seasons of our lives, and within our relationships. When these challenges come, you have a choice on how to respond. Our responses can be fear, sadness, numbness, anger, or anxiousness. When these responses affect our emotions, they ultimately affect how we make decisions. However, in this array of emotions and approaches to our choices, how do you seek God when challenges arise? More specifically, when there are health challenges, how do you gain confidence that God is even there when all the reports don't have a positive outlook? You may even question how and why this is happening either to you or a family member. How do you pray through these challenges?

If you read Romans 12:9-21, you see Paul explicitly lay out how those who believe in Christ should behave. He emphasizes that love, honor, being kind, and doing what is good is preferred. When you get to verse 12, he provides instructions on how to respond when we face challenges. Four actions stood out to me that proved to be prayer points as we seek God for a way through.

1. **Rejoice:** Have an attitude of gratitude. God is the same God today, yesterday, and forever more. How has he shown up in your life in the past?

2. **Be Confident:** Why are you lacking in the area of confidence? Is it fear, doubt, anxiety, or past experience? How will you allow your hope (*a feeling of expectation and desire for a certain thing to happen*) in God to be your anchor?

3. **Patience:** Be still; take time to just meditate and ask God for nothing. Just soak in His

presence and breath. We tend to hold our breath during challenges.

4. **Keep praying:** How will you remain faithful through this trail? Yes, keep praying. Not just for the things you need; pray for others. When we turn our attention to the needs of others, it allows our hearts to see God move in their lives, and we no longer must carry the anxiousness in our own life.

Facing Afflictions

Afflictions can be one of life's most difficult challenges from both the physical and spiritual perspectives. It can come out of nowhere and truly disrupt an individual's life and the life of those around them. What is an affliction? According to Merriam-Webster, affliction is **a** cause of persistent pain or distress, great suffering. As one can see, afflictions can be spiritual or physical. Examples of physical afflictions include the diagnosis of a disease, experiencing extreme mental suffering like depression,

One may view an affliction with a negative connotation; however, afflictions may come as a necessary test that leads us toward a greater purpose in our walk with God. Afflictions teach us to Rejoice in God, be confident in Him, be patient in it, and most importantly, keep praying.

"The Lord gets his best soldiers out of the highlands of affliction."

Charles Spurgeon

The Bible provides a significant number of stories of affiliations, what may have caused it, and, more importantly, how God intervened. During these times of affliction, we see that God is right there carrying us through, comforting us, and providing the sense we need to ultimately go back and help others who are experiencing the same thing.

Blessed be the God and Father of our Lord Jesus Christ, the Father of mercies and God of all comfort, who ***comforts us*** *in all our affliction, so that we may be able to* ***comfort those*** *who are in any affliction, with the comfort with which we ourselves are comforted by God.*

2 Corinthians 1:3-4, ESV

In 2013, I was faced with a challenge where I had to tap into the steps of "praying through." It was my daughter Jalynn's 12th birthday, and we were preparing to take a mini trip to New York City with her and her friend Indira. This trip included going to Manhattan, and Ellis Island, and bus tours around Harlem. We were all prepared and ready to go; however, that day, Jalynn had severe swelling in her knees like a balloon. We attributed this to basketball games and practices that took place that week, as she was on three different teams at that time. So, it was time to ice her up and get her on some ibuprofen.

I told the girls, "Get those knees down because if not, we are not going to be able to go."

So, these young ladies got themselves together and put ice packs on Jalynn's knees.

We woke up the next day; the knees seemed to be better as the swelling had gone down. And we made our way to New York City. We rolled the Greyhound bus all the way into Manhattan, me constantly checking and asking if our knees were okay, of course. Jalynn expressed she was okay, mainly because she wanted to keep going.

On the first day, we had a great time, went to the wax museum, and walked around town. We got on the tour bus that took us to various parts of the city; rode past the 911 Memorial and other attractions in New York. That night, we actually spent the night in the streets of New York City until about two o'clock in the morning; we went to Toys R Us and walked around the different stores. Just experiencing the nightlife and lights of Times Square was more than enough entertainment for two twelve-year-olds. However, by the next day, we noticed Jaylnn was unable to walk around without grimacing in pain. To alleviate that, we stayed on the tour bus for the entire day and toured the city, from Harlem to Greenwich Village to Columbia University and NYU.

At one point, I was carrying Jalynn on my back as we exited the tour bus; her knees were extremely stiff and not bending as normal. I was able to give her enough ibuprofen to do the Ellis Island tour, but we all knew this trip had to come to an end, and we had to press our way back to Massachusetts.

Lupus

A term and a diagnosis that I had unfortunately heard before because it had affected my grandmother and my mother, and we lost my sister before we could officially find out if she had it. In simple terms, Lupus is an autoimmune disease where the body attacks itself. A very complicated disease, as diagnosed patients may experience symptoms differently. This is what was determined to be the cause of Jalynn's initial pain that began on her 12th birthday. The rest of June and July was more basketball, summer camp, and swim lessons. She pressed her way through it; however, we began to notice the drastic weight loss, lack of appetite, and severe fatigue.

We went back and forth to the doctors a couple of times that summer, but no one could initially pinpoint what was going on. Finally, there was a breaking point; an ER visit and a demand placed on the doctors to figure out what was going on. A demand was made by my mother, and after one review of the blood work, my mother immediately said, "Check for Lupus."

The day of the potential diagnosis, a day of confusion, annoyance, and numbness. This was an interruption to the plans we had for my life. I was not sure how to comprehend what was taking place. I asked God why and how. What did I miss? Was I not attentive enough? We had already had this disease interrupt our lives enough times already. It has left so much grief and taken time away from what we desire to have in our lives. But here we are. However, this time was, in fact, different. God offered grace in this situation. We caught it in time. We were in the best place with the best medical care. We now know what it is; we know what words to use. Most importantly, we know how to pray.

That's what I tapped into, the power of prayer and intercession, also the power of prayer of those around me, true prayer warriors who would intercede on our behalf.

"Not this time," I said to the Lord.

I could sense my mother's fear and concern, but also her fight not to lose anyone else, nor no one else has to go through what she had gone through to get to where she had been health-wise at that moment.

Dealing with the What If!

Give all your worries and cares to God, for he cares about you.

1 Peter 5:7, NLT

This scripture can be a challenge if you know God or even His promises for your life. As women, we have an instinct to want to take care of or put some sort of control over a situation. When we do this, we have a sense of relief knowing that the specific plan we put in place will work. However, we only see in part. We do not know the future, and we fully don't know how it will all work out. And this is where the anxiety sets in. In turn, we will offer various scenarios in our heads to try to mitigate any distractions, hindrances, or failures. This is what keeps us up all night, the *WHAT IF*s!

But **WHAT IF** we truly "**Give all your worries**" to Him? The first step is to know that God cares for you deeply. Some of us have been put in the position of caretaker for so long that we do not even know what it feels like to be cared for. To know that God cares for you is to know what He says about you in His word. The second step is to know, without a doubt God loves us. And when someone loves us, they want to take care of us. We have a loving and caring God who does not want us to carry our worries, especially when we are concerned about someone facing affliction. His desire is to give them all to Him. How does one deal with the What ifs through prayer? Here is a suggested prayer action and reflection.

You must give ALL: what are you holding on to that you should be releasing to God? Are all your cares released to Him? Do you believe He cares for you? In your time of prayer, you must release them all to Him.

But by His Grace

But he said to me, "My grace is sufficient for you,
for my power is made perfect in weakness."
2 Corinthians 12:9 NIV

"His power is made perfect by my weakness." This phrase resonates with me in so many ways. Being very independent and somewhat of an introvert, I remember the times when I would not ask God for anything because I was always told God only helps those that help themselves. However, in 2 Corinthians 12:9, He makes it very clear that we do have weaknesses, and there is a grace that He gives us when we allow His power to work.

Although a lot of attention was needed to deal with Jalynn's diagnosis, God continues to show up in so many ways. Her treatments, her ability to go back to school and miss barely any days, me being about to take the time from work or even work while I am at the hospital. By that August, almost two months after her first symptoms, Jalynn was back playing basketball again. We did experience challenging days, but these were the days where God's grace, and His promise to care for us if we cast all our cares on him. Being confident in God's plan for her life would supersede this temporary affliction.

Resources

https://bestofchristianity.com/tag/types-of-affliction-in-the-bible/
https://www.rethinknow.org/meaning-of-romans-12-12/#:~:text=Even%20in%20the%20midst%20of,place%20your%20hope%20in%20Jesus.

Alicia Siryon-Wells

Minister Alicia Siryon-Wells has served the Lord in many capacities for the past twenty years with Advancing the Kingdom of God as her mandate. Alicia serves faithfully in the Ministry of Dance and has taught various workshops throughout the east coast. She is the Pageantry Director and course instructor for Moves of God (MOG) Global and the Co-Director for the National Liturgical Dance Network (NLDN), Massachusetts, and Rhode Island Chapters. In addition, she serves as the Associate Director and Minister for Living Water Outreach for Girls, Inc as well as the Board Treasurer and Prison Ministry Coordinator for Worship Arts Restoration (WAR).

Alicia released her first published book in 2021 called "Unashamed: Releasing the Power to Declare through Prayer." From that book, she birthed Unashamed 2 Declare Ministries; a ministry focused on Intercessory Prayer and being unashamed to declare the Gospel. Alicia resides in Massachusetts, where she engages in numerous community service and outreach initiatives across the region.

Alicia has her Bachelor of Science degree in Economics and Master of Science degree in Management Science from Bridgewater State University. She is the wife to William Wells, and mother to daughters, Jalynn and Jael.

For more information for booking engagement or to order any of her products or follow Minister

Alicia on all Social Media Platforms, please go to https://linktr.ee/unashamed2declare; or connect via email at unashamed2declare@gmail.com

Be Sober and Vigilant
By Nora Addison

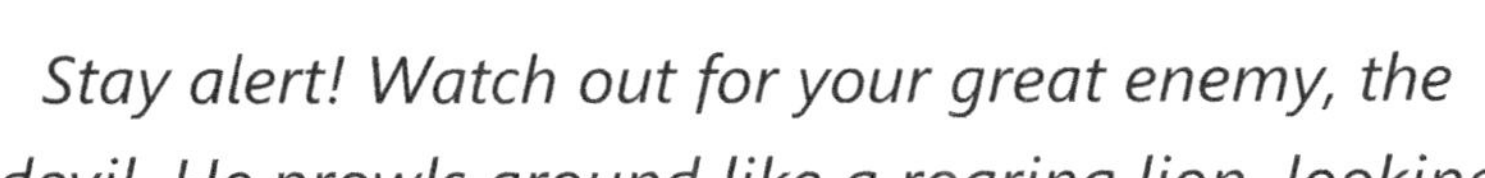

Stay alert! Watch out for your great enemy, the devil. He prowls around like a roaring lion, looking for someone to devour. -1 Peter 5:8

In August of 2021, crippling anxiety overtook my life. While I was showering, a thought came to my mind that I didn't know the answer to humanity's existence, how we got here, and what our purpose was; then, all of a sudden, this feeling came over me that I had never felt before let, alone explain. I felt like I had snapped out of a trance and knew there had to be more to this life rather than working to be successful and eventually dying and ever since that moment I started experiencing anxiety. It was hard to function throughout the day and talk to people like usual. And when I tried to seek help from those around me, they couldn't understand what I was talking about. Nights became horrifying, it'd be completely dark and silent throughout my house, and I'd be alone with fearful thoughts and thoughts about demons hiding behind my door or standing in the hallway. My nights were filled with hyperventilation, chest pain, brain burning, shivering, and overwhelming dread. Instead of sleeping, I watched guided walkthroughs on calming down from anxiety attacks or Bible meditations for fear. I'd think to myself, when is this going to end?

Will I ever be normal again and experience peace and joy from the little things? I can't do this anymore! I got on my knees desperately, begging GOD to take it away. I reached out to Him, saying what I heard in the Bible, "GOD, I'm on my knees; you said you created the heavens and earth, so surely you can take this anxiety away from me."

I cried to GOD, and the LORD listened; he saved me from all my troubles. When JESUS stepped into my situation, EVERYTHING changed! He told me that if I kept my mind on Him, He'd keep me in perfect peace Isa 26:3. I was desperate to be free from anxiety, so I did whatever it took to focus on JESUS, pushing through the crowd of distractions, discouragement, doubt, fear, and the devil's lies to touch the hem of His garment. I moved past distractions by cutting off anything that took my focus away from GOD. And I'd replace it with spending time with GOD, whether saturating in GOD's word, listening to a sermon, or fellowshipping.

When the devil came at me with thoughts of doubt and discouragement, I prayed GOD's word back to Him and reminded myself and the devil what GOD said in His word! JESUS told me in His word that If I keep my mind stayed on Him, He'll keep me in perfect peace, and all things are possible to those who believe! And although my situation may look and feel impossible, GOD said, "Behold, I am the GOD of all flesh. Is there anything too hard for me?"

Even when I felt fear trying to take over, I started to pray again, reminding GOD of His word just pouring out my heart, saying, "GOD, I can't do this. Can you strengthen me because I can't fight this battle myself. It's written in your word "be anxious for nothing but in everything by prayer with supplication let your request be made known to GOD, and the peace of GOD which surpasses all understanding shall guard your hearts and minds in Christ JESUS." And as much as the worry persisted, I was more persistent with repeating the promise of GOD.

I had to take captive every thought of fear and worry to the obedience of Christ (2 Corinth 10:5). I had to meditate on GOD's word rather than my problems, and I had to continue to trust him despite what it looked like. As I continued to seek JESUS and fill myself with His word, the spirit of fear was no longer present but a SPIRIT of power, love, and a SOUND MIND! GOD was faithful to His promise! He restored my peace and gave me joy, hope, rest for my mind and soul, and security. It's like I no longer had to worry about the things that unbelievers would worry about, like where we go when we die, preparing for the end of the world, or constantly being tormented by depression or anxiety. GOD has it all in His hands. It was the most fantastic feeling ever. I felt free, but it didn't last long.

Unfortunately, I got back in touch with some people from my past and got drawn back to everything I cut out to pursue JESUS (Proverbs 13:20). My friends saw how much I had changed and didn't mind being treated differently at first. I was just focused on sharing the hope, peace, joy, and freedom in JESUS, but my views slowly changed as I continued hanging out with them. I tried to hide JESUS as much as possible whenever I got around them because I didn't want to annoy them. I started to become discouraged with my walk with GOD and believed I was missing out on what the world had to offer. I was tired of being an outcast, so I started to partake in their worldly activities, which became a stumbling block in my relationship with GOD over time. I started making sacrifices for them by entertaining up sinful things, for instance, watching shows that broadcasted adultery and taking GOD's name in vain. I entertained inappropriate conversations and jokes that grieved the Holy Spirit. When I did this, I opened a door for the devil to come in; all that is in the world—the desires of the flesh, the desires of the eyes, and the pride of life—is not from the Father but from the world.

I didn't know how important it was to be equally yoked until I got into this mess. Christians cannot be partnered with unbelievers because their ways differ from GOD's. An unbeliever lives according to the flesh, and nothing good comes from it(Rom 7:18-19/Galatians 5:16-2). Although you may have used to be an unbeliever, we're called to leave behind the old ways and take up the new. At the same time, we are called to live according to the Spirit(Gal 6:8). And I realized the more I spent time with unbelievers, those who didn't believe in JESUS, the farther my heart got away from GOD(2 Corinthians 6:14)(Deut 7:3-4). And I say heart because although I was still reading the Bible not to get to know Him, I did out of obligation.

Before I knew it, not only was I dealing with anxiety, but I was also dealing with a mental stronghold. A mental stronghold is a lie that Satan has established in our thinking that we count as accurate but is a false belief. Since I had stopped spending time praying and studying GOD's word, I was vulnerable to the enemy's attacks. When I started spending quality time with GOD and reading His word, I noticed I was more reluctant to trust GOD and began to struggle with doubt; every time I'd read his word, I heard the devil whispering, "That's not true. How do you know if he's telling the truth? The Bible is manmade. You're being brainwashed."

I wanted to take GOD at his word because I knew that was the only way I could be at peace but no matter how hard I tried to give all my burdens to Him, I felt like I had no control to do that like something was hindering me, I became double-minded. And was unable to rest in the promises of GOD and could no longer be free from worry. I'd always pray to GOD, please forgive me and help my unbelief; please help me to have great faith despite what it takes, I don't want to live in bondage, but I want to be free like when you first saved me. And soon enough, GOD already had a plan for my situation. I started to see the word fast everywhere, and I didn't understand it at first until, one night, I was walking to the gas station to get some snacks, and as we were leaving, I saw this lottery machine. The thing I noticed was fast and pray. Then I heard, "This kind comes out but by fasting and praying." The screen reads fast and play, but after I read fast and pray. From there, GOD began to lead me on many fasts, but I became discouraged and angry because I felt like I wasn't progressing. GOD led me to the song "Don't lose heart" by Steven, and I can say today that GOD is fighting my battles! I no longer struggle with double-mindedness and anxiety.

GOD has the final say. He's on the throne, not you, your fears, your parents, or the devil! He didn't leave me in my mess. I surely thought it was the end for me that I was hopeless, But GOD, through this trial, although it was tough, I now know that there's power in prayer, and despite what your situation looks like, all things are possible to those who believe. Even when you fall into a pit, there's no situation that GOD won't be able to pull you out of as long as you remain in His word and trust in Him.

Nora Addison

Nora Addison spreads the good news about JESUS and tells others of the hope in Him. Nora plans on using her passion, graphic designing, to tell her story and further His Kingdom. However, she hasn't always been like this; When COVID-19 spread, her state and many other states got issued into quarantine; As death reports started to rise, the fear of death persuaded her to seek GOD. She started reading the Bible, praying daily, and fasting. All of it was done out of obligation. God wanted intimacy, a relationship, not religion. It wasn't about fasting to fast or reading to read but reading to learn who your creator is and getting to know Him. And in August 2021, GOD showed her what it meant to experience a relationship with Him, rather than religion.

I just returned from spending the day with my family and friend and hopped in the shower. As I was soaping up, I thought, "Why and how did I get here." And suddenly, I felt like I was out of my body. My heart started to race; I hurried out of the shower believing if I lay down, the feeling would go away, but it got worse. I felt symptoms of anxiety, intense shaking, sweaty palms, and diarrhea. So, I got on my knees and prayed, "GOD, I don't want to die; I don't know what's happening; I need your help because I can't do this; please take this away!" I knew I needed Him at that moment. The Holy Spirit led me on YouTube, which I didn't know at the time, to bible verses about anxiety. Just by holding onto His promises allowed me to sleep that night. The following day, I told my family what was happening, but they didn't know what I was talking about and thought I was fine. It became hard to function throughout the day. I had trouble eating, working, showering, sleeping at night; I even started experiencing brain-burning anxiety. Until one night. I got invited to a clubhouse room called "Speak Life," and a Prophet of GOD spoke life over me, "If you keep your mind on GOD, He'll keep you in perfect peace." The next day I listened to the audio Bible, still remembering what the Prophet told me last night.

I wanted my peace back severely, so I held onto GOD's promise every time the anxiety would come upon me, and I would remind GOD of what HE said; by the end of the day, GOD fulfilled what HE said AND MORE. Over time, He restored my peace and gave me joy, a purpose, the will to live, and the ability to function again! And when I found out that GOD and His word were true. I read the Bible at every chance and became on fire with the passion for telling people and those who feel hopeless, misunderstood, and unheard. Your situation may seem impossible, but it's not for GOD! He's the answer! That's not my belief, but it's the truth! He's the truth, the way, and the life. If He did it for me, He'd do it for you!

If you ever have any questions, feel free to contact me on my personal account @lets_b.woke.if you'd like design work done or would like to see my design work, my business account is @ncreatess.

Restoring Faith: Redeeming Love and Rejoicing in Life! By Rachelle Love

Our project is appropriately named The Love Factor, featuring a combination of unique real-life stories from women from all walks of life. Having an intimate relationship with your creator, the one true and living God, is an incredible experience. Father God is truly the missing component in many people's lives. He sent His only begotten Son, Jesus Christ, to redeem mankind from spiritual death and restore abundant life. Jesus is the Love Factor.

When we reflect on God's goodness and mercy, that never fails, yet His love endures forever. What a mighty God we serve. It's hard to even fathom that this invisible yet very tangible God is present in our daily lives. His touch is ever so gentle; He whispers our name to our mothers and fathers before we are even born. He has told us in His world in Jeremiah 1:5, "Before I formed you in the womb, I knew you; Before you were born, I sanctified you; I ordained you a prophet to the nations."

My story gives a flashback to seven years ago, in 2016. After celebrating my 50th birthday, two months later, I suffered a sudden cardiac arrest and died on my living room floor. Boom! There was no warning; I didn't say a word. What was so significant about my story and journey? This was not my end, but only the start of something so transformative it could only be described as a true miracle...more details to come later in my story.

One of my favorite scriptures is Jeremiah 29:11

"For I know the thoughts that I think towards you, says Yahweh, thoughts of peace and not of evil, to give you hope and a future, you shall call on me, and you shall go and pray to me, and I will listen to you."

Sometimes, the uncertainty in life is what scares us. Fear, doubt, and unbelief will creep in. We must get to the root of whether we trust God fully or can we overcome whatever obstacle we must face. He tells us in Romans 8:28, "And we know that all things work together for our good to them that love God, who are the called according to His purpose.

We may not feel that we are prepared to deal with accidents, natural disasters, or sudden death. When we experience disappointments, setbacks, loss, or heartbreaks, God is right there with us. What are the first questions that come to mind? We often question God, like, Father, why did this terrible thing happen? How will I recover, or will I survive it? One key principle to walking with God, one must have faith. Where is your faith? My walk with God started at an early age; it helped to shape my spiritual understanding. It's funny; when you are young in the Lord, and you pray for something, it usually happens quickly.

God's unfailing love supersedes circumstances; His love can give your life, strength, and power. The act of praying is direct communication with Father God. Jesus teaches us that when we pray, He gives us an example, which we have come to know as The Lord's prayer. Jesus lets us know in *John 17:7, "If you abide in me, and my words abide in you, ask for whatever you wish, and it will be done for you.*" He wants our lives to bear much fruit, so shall ye be my disciples, followers of Christ. Let His word resonates with our spirits by taking one day at a time to spend time with Father God by reading and refreshing your spirit daily. You are renewing your mind; therefore, we take on the spirit of God. When we speak or pray about a certain thing, we will begin to experience peace in that matter, and confidence rises!

Further, Jesus teaches us according to *Matthew 6:9-13 (KJV). After this manner, therefore, pray ye: Our Father, which art in heaven. Hallowed by thy name. Thy kingdom comes, thy will be done in earth, as in heaven. Give us this day our daily bread, and forgive us our debts, as we forgive our debtors. And lead us not into temptation but deliver us from evil: For thine is the kingdom, and the power, and the glory, forever. Amen.*

As we develop our prayer life, praying or talking with the Lord becomes natural. Understanding there are several types of prayer, you should understand when to use them and why.

1. Prayer of Worship
2. Prayer of Thanksgiving
3. Prayer of Faith
4. Prayer of Intercession
5. Corporate Prayer
6. Consecration
7. Prayer of the Holy Spirit.

The key to having your prayers answered is to believe in your heart that God is, and He can do whatever you ask. You build confidence when seeking the Lord for advice or if you desire certain things to happen. The foundation of prayer can begin as a young child blessing our food and saying prayers at night.

I can remember when I was about seven years old, in the second grade, I accepted Jesus as my personal Lord and Savior. I was still very young, but I had a zeal for the things of the Lord. I was baptized and started serving as a junior usher in my local church. When I look back over my life, I can say God has been faithful to me, not because I did anything special, but because His love was always there.

Our relationship must be solid with Father God. He must be the first place in our lives. We cannot allow distractions in this world. If we allow other things to take first place in our lives, we will begin to put our focus or confidence in those things instead of God. Our confessions are very powerful. *Proverbs 18:21 tells us Death and life are in the power of the tongue.* So, why do people say all kinds of things that are contrary to the word of God?

I wanted to give you the backstory, so you could understand my journey. Speaking faith is a lifestyle. As you become aware of God's word, you will begin to believe in God for finances, healing, protection, and peace. I want to share this story; when my younger sister and I were attending a church, the minister would often call us up to the front to sing a Christian song by Phil & Brenda Nicholas. The funny thing is the title of the song was Got to Tell Somebody, just can't keep it to Myself, what the Lord has done for Me. It was a song that only adults could relate to since both of us were grade school-aged, eight and ten years old. They spoke of sinful ways, job loss, sickness, and so on. It wasn't until we both got older. We were married with children of our own. Soon, we started experiencing layoffs, sickness then we could understand how good God was to us and our own families.

The following scenarios are a series of my testimonies that allowed me to increase my faith by confessing God's word daily and renewing my mind. Part of my daily confession consisted of this prayer. Jesus has redeemed me from the curse of the law; cursed was everything that hung on a tree. Poverty, sickness, and disease are not my portion. God has left an inheritance for me and my children, according to Deuteronomy 28:1-14. The evil one has no authority over me or my family. The Greater one lives inside me than he that is in the world. Lord, thank you for making me the head, and not the tail, above only and not beneath. I shall live and not die and proclaim the works of the Lord. Hallelujah!

As we matured, several situations gave us pause, but we did not panic or lose heart. We were used to praying over ourselves in the morning before we would leave for school. "No weapon formed against us shall prosper; this does not mean weapons would not be formed, only they could not prosper against us.

One day after school, my sister and I were on our way home, and we decided to stop by the neighborhood liquor store for some snacks. While we were inside the store, standing by the cold drink cooler, I turned and noticed a robbery was in place; a man was holding a gun. I immediately shielded my sister and told her to be quiet; we both began to pray in our heavenly language. I could hear the gunman yell to everyone to come to the front of the store. We knelt on the floor, and while our eyes were closed, I felt the young man walk right by us as if he did not see us.

Just like that, the robbery was over the gunman, and his accomplice got away. The police were called, and we ran out of the store all the way home, not even purchasing our intended snacks. My sister recalled that we did not pray Psalm 91 that morning, but she had covered us later in the day. Once again, we marvel at the faithfulness of God; this situation could have ended tragically.

While expecting the youngest of my three children, I was rushed into emergency surgery for a C-section; I was in my eighth month of pregnancy. The entire ordeal was scary, but my faith in God was strong. I knew He would see us through it, my baby was delivered safely, and he stayed in the NIC-Unit for about two weeks. His birth weight was only 3 lbs. 4 ounces.

One summer afternoon, the temperatures had reached over 100 degrees; my ex-husband accidentally left our youngest child in the car, still buckled in his car seat; he was just under one year old. The entire afternoon, my baby was in this hot car, but the faithfulness of God prevailed again. Angels cooled my son while he slept; we discovered him and cooled him off with wet towels.

I've shared these incredible yet painful passages in my life to offer hope in a hopeless situation. To promote faith whenever you lack faith. To encourage the greatest experience of love. *For God so loved the world, that He gave His only begotten Son, that whosoever shall believe in Him, shall not perish, but have everlasting life. John 3:16.*

Remember, a test is just a journey until you get to the other side of the mountain to make it a testimony! Jesus said, whosoever shall speak to the mountain, and tell it to be removed and cast into the sea and shall not doubt in his heart but shall believe those things which he says shall come to pass. He shall have whatever he says. What mountains are hanging around in your lives? Allow Father God to work through your life by using these confessions right out of the word of God. So, then faith comes by hearing and hearing the word of God.

I am truly a miracle survivor. I not only want to survive, but I want to thrive and impact others' lives. They can live their best lives as well! Our marvelous God will not forsake you. There is a great reward if we don't faint or give up. Continue to praise and give Him thanksgiving daily for what He has already done. *Hebrews 11:1 says, now faith is the substance of things hoped for, the evidence of things not seen. When we stand in our truth, being authentic and relatable, it gives others hope, faith, and love, that God can do exactly what He promised to do. He is truly a way maker, a promise keeper.*

I want my life to be a living example of what God can do through a person's life. I am rewinding my original testimony from the beginning. In May

2016, two months after celebrating my fifty-birthday, I experienced a sudden cardiac arrest, and I died on my living room floor. My husband was alerted by the Holy Spirit to go check on your wife. He immediately got up and came into the living room, where I lay lifeless, unresponsive, and not breathing. My husband called 9-1-1 and was instructed to do CPR. Within 5 minutes, the EMTs arrived. They were unable to revive me as I had no pulse. Using the defibrillator three times, my heart started pumping again; they rushed me to the hospital. Doctors wanted to preserve my brain function, so they immediately placed me into a medically induced coma for 72 hours. This may have seemed like the longest three days of our lives. I was unaware of what had taken place. My mother, sister, and children were doing a prayer vigil around the clock.

Finally, the time came to start warming my body, as I was on life-support, and the machines were breathing for me. When the Doctor called my name, I did not respond. When my mom called my name, I awoke. Still very groggy, the doctor explained what happened to me. I was transferred to another hospital for rehab to learn to walk again; three weeks had passed since this incident.

Two years after my traumatic situation, my husband of 15 years transitioned. I was fortunate; God allowed me to spend those last two weeks with him while he was hospitalized. We had closure and made peace with each other; he left me with a special message. That I will always cherish, he understood why the Lord allowed me to come back from death, and that was to care for him during his transition.

Today, I celebrate victory daily when I wake up. He didn't have to allow me to see another day as it was not yet my time. I was given another chance; the Spirit of God spoke to me while I was recovering. He said the place where I lay dead is the same; I made an altar to Him. I had a prayer partner; we each would pray every morning at 5:30 am. These were the good seeds that were sown on behalf of others' intercession.

The Lord supernaturally imparted a purpose and passion; now, my life has a God-driven purpose. My life aligns with my purpose, and I'm eternally grateful for the opportunity to share this message of hope, love, and redemption.

It's been seven years, in God's timing; it's called completion, since the incident. I'm writing my story to let others know God cares for all of us and loves us very deeply. It's according to your faith, be it unto you. He is not a respecter of people, but what pleases Him is when we use our faith because everyone has been given the same measure of faith.

It's time to activate your faith and start exercising faith, with the small things like believing in God for a parking space in a crowded mall. Asking God for a favor when you are applying for a new job. Or you when you need a financial breakthrough. God is in the healing business. He is our provider, according to Philippians 4:19 But my God shall supply all my need according to His riches and glory by Christ Jesus. God is our healer, Jehovah Rapha, according to Isaiah 53:4. Surely, He has borne our griefs and carried our diseases, yet we accounted Him stricken and smitten by God, and afflicted. But He was wounded for our transgressions, crushed for our iniquities; upon

Him was the punishment that made us whole by His stripes; we were healed.

Please allow me to say a special prayer for anyone seeking renewal in their faith, believing in God for the manifestation of healing or a financial breakthrough.

Father God, I come boldly to your throne room, giving you praise and glory. Thank you for allowing me to share my testimony of your wonderful works. Your word tells believers in Joshua 1:8 to meditate on your word day and night, to observe to do according to all that is written therein: for then thou shall make thy way prosperous, and he shall have success!

If anyone is believing you for their loved ones to come into the fold, Father, I ask for laborers to be sent to the highways and byways to compel them to come to Jesus. For those believing in a financial blessing, I set myself in agreement with their faith. It is faith that pleases you. I rejoice in advance for all the blessings that you will bestow on these individual saints. Thank you, Father God, for your goodness and mercy that greets us daily. Your word shall remain as you hasten over your word to perform that where it was sent! Let hearts be changed, softened, and ears open to hear your word.

Thank you for the answer in Jesus' mighty name, Amen.

Rachelle Love, MBA

Rachelle Love

Rachelle Love, MBA touts over two decades of professional business development management, coaching, and consulting experience. Rachelle has worked with top Fortune 500 companies. She has exceptional expertise in building brands, developing creative promotional and marketing materials, event planning, styling, and project management. Her work history includes industries such as financial services, Big-5 accounting firms, legal and real estate.

Love is a leader who is now transforming our community of female business owners and entrepreneurs, by infusing financial literacy education. We are vertically integrated, utilizing real estate investing, coaching, and personal and business funding to help you grow, scale, and leverage your business and relationships. For 10 years, Love served as Principal and Managing Director of The Fabuluxe Agency. As a boutique consulting firm, it was specially designed for the melanin woman. Small business owners sought her coaching services, to develop their voice and signature style in the marketplace. Operating as a trusted advisor and strategic partner, Rachelle quickly found an untapped niche, she began working with distinguished clientele in media, entertainment, and the nonprofit sectors.

However, in 2016, her life took a drastic turn as she suffered a life-threatening medical emergency, which halted all business activities. Then, in 2018, she experienced a devastating personal loss; her husband of 15 years passed away. Picking up the broken pieces of her life, God's divine favor graced her life and allowed Love to blossom again.

Love is a California native and resides in Los Angeles with her family. Her hobbies include reading, biking and dancing.

info@rachellelove.com

www.rachellelove.com | 833.442.5899

Applying Prayer Power to the Process
By Norma Iris Medina

Confess your faults one to another, and pray one for another, that ye may be healed. The effectual fervent prayer of a righteous man availeth much.
James 5:16, KJV

My heart was palpitating, my hands were sweating, my stomach was in knots, and I kept saying to myself, "Please do not pick me, please do not pick me!" With my shoulders stooped and head bowed down, it might have appeared to some that I was crouched over, resembling the hunchback of Notre Dame. Or, hopefully, others would believe I was immersed in His presence. I peeked with one eye, hoping no one would make eye contact with me, simultaneously observing to see if someone else volunteered to go next in our prayer circle at church. I started counting the number of people in our circle, hoping we would run out of time. Upon initially joining, I thought I was just going to be a quiet member of the prayer team, pray in silence and come into agreement with the others. But now the team was engaging in "popcorn" style prayer, where after one person on the team would finish praying, the next person would proceed, and so on. I was petrified! Long story short, I overcame the fear and prayed.

That was about 20 years ago when I first rededicated my life to God. At first, I was clueless about how to pray and what to pray for. Initially, I thought prayers were recited from the King James Version, which, honestly, I could not grasp. I chuckle at how complicated I made prayer to be. But I was what I thought was a hopeless case. Determined to figure out this prayer thing, I went to a Christian book store, back when going to a physical Christian book store was a thing. We were not in the digital age yet.

I remember the moment I walked into the store like it happened yesterday. I smiled at the cashier, and she smiled back brightly. With hunger within and the desperation to learn how to pray, I mustered the courage to ask the salesperson if she could recommend any prayer books. Needless to say, I left the bookstore with a jackpot of treasures, and thus my prayer journey began. In reading the recommended books, I learned that prayer was basically talking with God. What a simple concept! I thought. I already knew how to talk to Him, so had I been "praying" all that time? I guessed I just needed some fine-tuning.

I decided to start by reading two prayer books I had purchased, "The Power of A Praying Wife" and "The Power of A Praying Parent," both by Stormie Omartian. She had written beautiful prayers outlined with scriptures and fill-in blanks to write loved ones' names. I held those books close to my heart as I did my Bible. I began learning Bible verses and prayed them back to God. This caused me to gain momentum and God-given confidence. I begin to see the Lord answer many prayers. One of the first was my desire to attend a women's retreat at my church, but my unbelieving husband made things a bit challenging for me.

After one Sunday service, an elder of the church hugged me, whispering in my ear, "The Lord told me to give this to you... I do not know why, but I am being obedient."

I nodded and said, "Thank you," and she

walked away.

I opened my hand, and it was the exact dollar amount I needed to register for the women's retreat. I was in tears and overjoyed. Encouraged and overwhelmed with gratitude, my faith was strengthened to keep praying for bigger things and believing in God for more. I kept praying for my family and others. And there were countless moments God tremendously used to build my faith and cause me to enter into deeper levels of intimacy with Him. One morning at work, my co-worker was experiencing a severe headache, and I asked her if she would like me to pray for her. She did not hesitate, and before I spoke a word, I asked her, "Do you believe you can be healed?" She nodded.

I laid hands on her head, and she was instantly healed, almost falling back when the anointing of God hit her. Over the years, I prayed for many people, whether I knew them or not, and witnessed many answered prayers. I prayed for my family's salvation, healing, deliverance, restoration, and whatever issues, challenges, or crises that arose. I was on fire for God and wanted everyone to experience the same fire and love I had for the

Father and people. Years later, I worked for a children's hospital as a medical coder. A few of my family members, including my dad, also worked at the hospital. One afternoon, my dad came to my office and asked if I would come and join him to see a little girl who was given a bad report; he wanted to know if I was willing to pray for her. When we arrived at this beautiful baby girl's room, she was hooked up to way too many machines and monitors. My father was a respiratory technician and had formed a bond with the girl's parents' families.

My father introduced me to the baby's mother. As I spoke to her, I could see the pain in her eyes as she began to explain her daughter's medical condition. I asked if she would allow me to pray for her baby, and she agreed. As I began to pray, my father came to an agreement. Afterward, I encouraged the mom with a kind word and returned to my office. Shortly after some days of praying, we received a praise report that the little girl was healed and discharged to go home. The mom wanted to see me, and when we spoke, it was a great jubilee! I invited her to come to my church. To my surprise, she testified of God's goodness in front of the congregation! I couldn't help but delight in God's goodness.

As I served God more, I realized that prayer was more than just talking to God. It is believing Him in His word. It is trusting that His Word will not return void to Him and that His promises are yes and amen for us! Prayer coupled with humility and repentance can move us in such a way to see His hand over a situation. Sometimes we may not see our prayers answered due to one or several elements blocking the flow of blessings from navigating their way to us. Within us may be underlying unforgiveness, bitterness, resentment, traumas, hatred, unbelief, and so on.

Let me encourage you: in spite of your internal struggles within, please do not give up praying. Keep pressing through! Just because it has not happened yet or there is a delay does not mean you have been denied. Just because God has not answered yet does not mean that you should stop praying. His timing is perfect, and as He has done in my life, He builds strength, hope, and patience within us. God has taught me that the process is necessary and to embrace it. We can't opt out of it, or like what I tried doing at one season of particular hardship, check out of life, coasting on autopilot. If you live on this earth and are human, you will have trouble. The Word of God says, “I have told you these things, so that in me you may have peace. In this world you will have trouble. But take heart! I have overcome the world.” (John 16:33, NIV)

There was a time when my prayer life was tested by long-suffering. I had rededicated my life back to Jesus when I was about five years into my marriage with two children, and my life was upside down. I was stressed with marriage, challenged by my kids, and several ongoing situations that honestly motivated me to go back to church. I had previously left because of the pain I experienced within the church with my family. How amazing how he would bring me back to receive healing from where I was wounded. In 1999, I was praying to God and believing in Him for many things, despite not truly walking in the ways of the Lord. Nevertheless, despite my flaws and sin, I still trusted God and walked by faith. I know it may sound strange, but I've learned not to limit God by limiting myself. My husband and I were in the process of searching for a two-flat building (a building with two apartments) for purchase. We were not having much luck or help from our realtor.

We had just seen another broken-down dwelling that, in my mind, should not have been on the market, to begin with. Choosing to fight discouragement with faith, I told my husband while he was driving not to worry. "We will find our own home," I assured him. As soon as those words poured out of my mouth, I instantly heard the Holy Spirit say, Turn left here. I was not surprised because I had heard God speak to me since I was in the sixth grade. I just never shared it with anyone because I didn't think anyone would believe me. Immediately, we turned left, and behold, as soon as we turned, there was the beautiful two-flat brick building we had been hoping and praying for.

The best part was that it was being sold by the owner with no middleman. I had my husband double-park so that I could write down the phone number. My stomach was filled with butterflies, and both my husband and I left with smiles, encouraged. My husband, to my surprise, left me in charge of calling, meeting, and, eventually, negotiating. It was a God thing from start to finish because my husband prided himself in handling any type of finances and business-related projects for the family. Probably even more to my surprise, I ran with it. I had done my homework and researched everything I needed to know about the property, area, and housing industry at that time.

It was a buyer's market, and we went into this house-shopping adventure by faith without yet being pre-approved for a loan. We met directly with the owner, Mr. Jim Salvi, and we found out his father had built the house we came to look at, as well as the other houses on that block. As we continued to tour the property, we went outside to the backyard, and I pictured our two kids playing outside. It brought such a gentle warmth. We came back inside, and I examined every nook and cranny of the building. As I was inspecting the home, I found that it was kept in immaculate condition! It was the best home out of all the others we looked at by far.

In my head, I was calculating and deducting what the cosmetic work would cost us to remodel the home. Prior to us viewing the property, we came up with a figure that we felt was reasonable and beneficial for both parties. With this, we also did our own comparison analysis on what other homes had sold and were selling for in the area. God gave us the plan and strategy. This was our first time buying a property, and we were learning as we went along in this exploit on which God was leading. It came time to negotiate, and the owner did not want to budge on his price point. He was firm on the asking price. I reminded him of all the work we would have to do to update the outdated kitchen and finish the unfinished basement. Still, he would not relent. I stood firm amidst a long silence.

As the owner refused to negotiate and we prepared to leave, I exclaimed, "Our offer still stands! Please call us if you reconsider." We exchanged numbers and left. I prayed about it, but after six months had passed, we still had not heard anything back from him. We decided to take a drive by the property to check if it was still available, but to our dismay, the "Sale by Owner" sign was no longer on the lawn. I questioned my discussion tactics and asked my husband if I was too strong or hard in my negotiation.

"No," he reassured me. "You did what needed to be done." His affirmation did make me feel somewhat better, but I still found myself asking why. Why did it not happen the way we hoped? Why would God send us there?

At this point, we needed to figure out something quick as my father-in-love was selling his building, and we lived in the apartment above my husband's dad. One evening, I got a call, and when I answered, I heard a gentleman ask me, "Is this Iris?" I responded, "Yes." He proceeded to talk and say, "Hi, Iris, this is Jim Salvi. I own the property you came out to see."

I was shocked and flabbergasted! He began to ask me, "Are you still interested in buying the property?"

I was stunned, to say the least, so to make sure I heard correctly, I asked him if he could please give me the property's address, for we had seen so many properties, and I did not want to jump the erroneous gun. My heart gave a sigh of relief when he confirmed the address. I told Jim that we were under the impression that he sold the property because we no longer saw the "For Sale" sign on the lawn.

The owner responded, "Oh, we took it off because we travel back and forth to Florida."

Jim accepted our offer! Hallelujah! But then

we had a problem! Well, a good problem. We still needed to get approved for a loan. Can you believe that the offer we provided the buyer was for the exact amount we got approved? You can't tell me God did not answer! Our closing day was successful and went graciously well. We moved in, and we had our third child a year later.

One day as I was returning from work, I was in Fullerton when the Lord had me look out of the car window to my right. I saw a church sign with the name Bethesda. I shouted in the car, "That cannot possibly be the church I grew up in! The last time I attended was such a long time ago!" To be exact, it had been about 13 years since I left as a teenager and returned, married with three kids. What brought me to the feet of Jesus was not wanting to live this life without Him.

At that point in my life, I was hungry, lonely, hurt, and desperate for Jesus. Also, my father had given me a book to read, and I had to confess to him that I had procrastinated in reading it for about two years because it literally scared me. The book was "The Divine Revelation of Hell" by Catherine Baxter.

As I can recall my dad saying, "Mama, before

you read the book, pray to God to take the fear away because fear is not from God'" I did as he suggested, and I was not afraid. I looked for the book in our new place and found it. I read the testimony of the author, and I saw nothing but the compassion of Jesus throughout the book. I was touched by His heart, and it moved me to tears. I repented and surrendered my life to Jesus that day.

At that moment, I felt a great relief and peace that I had not experienced before, and when my husband arrived home, I told him that I had given my life to the Lord. I also let him know that if he wanted to ask me anything, I was ready to sincerely answer any questions and confess anything he liked to know.

With a solemn expression, he answered, "No." That no was the starting point of my juggling two worlds as I continued to partner in life with him: the life of an unsaved husband living with a saved wife.

I spoke with God and said, "Lord, if my husband prevents me from serving You, then I must go."

Though my husband did not understand the change in me, and he did not like it at first, he eventually warmed up to it about a decade later. And boy, did he give me a lot of grief. I could not understand it then, but he felt he was competing with God for me.

My husband was willing to stay in the marriage, and the Lord showed me a scripture regarding how a Christian wife should live with a difficult husband so that he would be attracted to Christ by her behavior.

1 Corinthians 7:13, NIV tells us, "If any woman has a husband who is an unbeliever, and he consents to live with her, she should not divorce him." I was not in any physical danger, just incredibly challenged, so we stayed married, but divorce was brought up by me more than once. Fast forward years later, I was still praying for my husband with one of my dear friends who, along with me, was on the prayer team at our church in Joliet. She knew my marital struggles and prayed with me through some highly difficult times. With every chance we could get, my kids and I would invite my husband to church as much as we could, mainly when the kids would perform for the holidays in singing and plays and when our daughters would dance with the worship dance

team.

Once in a while, he would accompany us, but for a long time, I took our then ten kids to church by myself. To my embarrassment, someone at the church who didn't know us assumed I was single! Yes, life was difficult, and it got even worse when God called us to move to Las Vegas over a decade later.

My husband stayed behind to complete the sale of our family home we had in Coal City, Illinois. I packed the kids up in our 15-passenger van, stuffed with our belongings, along with a trailer that, as we drove, would only allow us to do the bare minimum speed on the highway. My 18-year-old daughter helped me to drive our other minivan. We left in such a rush that there was no time to get a tune-up for both vans. All we had for the kids, and myself were the lunches we packed and my last check from my job. I felt anxiety getting the best of me while we were on the road, so I decided to stop at a nearby gas station and pray.

That is when my oldest daughter, MJ, who lived in Texas, called me on my cell and asked, "Mom, what state will you stop and book a hotel?"

I chuckled, "Um, MJ, we are driving all the way straight through." There was a long pause after that. We hung up, and a few minutes afterward, she called me back. "Mom, what if you pick me up in one of the states you're driving through and scoop me at one of the airports? I want to help you drive." I was stunned at her kind offer and gladly accepted. We calculated the time and state where we would be, down to the precise location, and we scooped her up at the Nebraska airport. MJ helped us drive the remaining 16 hours to Las Vegas. She was a godsend. Even though my husband had stayed behind for a bit to tie up loose ends with our previous home, we were on bad terms before I hit the road with the kids because of the high-stress levels of getting everything together for the move, especially trying to do all this during the Covid-19 pandemic. We barely communicated. When the kids and I finally arrived at our new home, we were exhausted, and it took us at least three months to recover from the emotional overload.

My husband and I were trying to do the best we knew how and dealing with unexpected setbacks. I lived in Las Vegas with the kids for almost a year and dealt with everything like a single mom. (I will divulge the details in my next book.) But God met us at the place where our hearts were. He saved our family from destruction. He delivered my husband and me from divorce and brought forth healing, deliverance, restoration, and salvation in Las Vegas, baby! Out of all places, Las Vegas! Won't He do it?

My husband gave his life to the Lord, and we are now in ministry together. Was it easy? Heck no! But when is anything worth doing ever easy? Was it possible? Not with man, but yes, it was possible with God. In His Word, Jesus said, "...With man this is impossible, but with God all things are possible." (Matthew 19:26, ESV) If you are reading this, be encouraged. God has not forgotten you. You are His beloved, and He loves you with everlasting love. Stay the course in prayer. He will make it worth your while.

Norma Iris Medina

Norma Iris Medina was born and raised in the Windy City of Chicago. Norma is passionate about praying and helping others. She is a certified Christian Mental Health Coach, teacher, speaker, wife, and mom to ten wonderful children. Her Advocacy is for children & families. She resides in Las Vegas with her kids and husband of Thirty- plus years. Norma's heart is for the Nations; she loves traveling with her family.

March 3, 2023 "Confess your faults one to another, and pray one for another, that ye may be healed. The effectual fervent prayer of a righteous man availeth much.
James 5:16

My Journey to the Father
By Monique Baker

And I will be your Father, and you will be my sons and daughters, says the Lord Almighty.
2 Corinthians 6:18

My life up until the writing of this excerpt has been filled with doubt, worry, and all that comes with those things. Oh yes, I was and am a believer, but I was dealing with hurts I tried to ignore in hopes they would disappear. But these hurts were inhibiting me from moving forward to live a life of freedom in Christ Jesus. The hurt made it difficult for me to trust God. It was something hard to admit because I love the Lord so much.

One day during a session preparing for this writing, I had a breakthrough. The writing session turned into a session of revelation and deliverance. The session connected the dots for me. It only revealed my trust issue; God saw fit to show me where it started. Thus began my journey to surrender to my Father God. My mindset began transforming, and my prayer life has taken on a whole different meaning. I feel like a butterfly coming out of a cocoon. Let me share my journey.

Be ye transformed by the renewing of your mind.
Romans 12:2

I did not realize that one of the key reasons for my lack of trust in God came from the departure of my earthly father when I was a child. Before I go any further, I want to state that I never considered that the non-existence of my dad's presence affected me in any way, nor did I feel any deep anger towards him for it. Did I have moments when I disliked him? Absolutely, but the negative impact never crossed my mind. However, as I began to reflect, one thing stood out from a child until now: I've always desired the feeling of being safe or protected.

This desire as a child began to be fulfilled for me when my mother accepted Christ as her Savior, and we started attending a church far different from the catholic church we went to. The day I stepped into the church as a little girl, I still remember thinking that my life would never be the same again. The desire to feel safe and protected was at church when we would have all-night prayer, three-day shut-ins, and church convocations. Whenever the churches we fellowshipped with got together, I felt so much joy...I felt safe.

As I grew older, I began to desire more of God; I didn't want to keep doing the wrong things. So, I decided I was going to accept Christ as my Lord and Savior during the annual youth conference. That I did; however, it didn't stick. I'd find myself the following Monday after the youth conference not feeling saved. So, I tried again during the next youth conference, the next one, and so on and so on. Eventually, I noticed the saints would mention "the keeping power." That's what I was missing! So, I sought after the "keeping power," which is the Holy Spirit for those that may not know. I sought after the Holy Spirit and received the Holy Spirit. That day the sun was extra bright, and if you asked me how I felt, I would have said, "Just call me the demon slayer." I was on top of the world, me, my Savior, and the Holy Spirit.

Well went to church the evening I received the Holy Spirit, and much happened that night that was devastating, broke my joyful spirit, and led me to believe that I did not have the Holy Spirit, but I was possessed by a demon. The only thing I could think was, why didn't you protect me? Why did you allow this to happen to me? I left church service that night numb.

Even now, I can't tell you where I went after church or who I was with. My world crashed around me because the place I felt the safest and the God I wanted didn't protect me from being hurt. I felt like an outsider that was evil from that time on. I didn't want to be around the saints because I felt like an extremely bad person that God didn't care about. I felt ostracized and abandoned. Now I know that was a lie, but as a young person at that time, I didn't know.

I will never leave you nor forsake you. Hebrews 13:5

When I became older, I left the church and ran the streets, searching for someone to love me and make me feel protected. Someone I could trust, someone that would be there for me when I needed them. However, the odd thing was that I didn't recognize it even if I found someone like that. It didn't seem to ever be enough. It wasn't quite what I desired. After all the running, I found myself back in church, and the most beautiful thing happened. I went up for prayer, and the person that prayed for me said Lord let her feel your love tangibly. At that very moment, I literally felt arms wrap around me that felt so warm and consoling; I felt the words "I Love You." From that time until I finally decided to stop running completely, whenever I visited a church, I could feel God's love envelop me like a glove.

When I finally settled myself and joined a church, the one God sent me to had members displaying the level of love I needed. From the Pastor to the ushers, the love in the church was amazing.

Although there was love all around me, I still had difficulty surrendering myself to God fully. I sang on the praise team and worked with youth. I was active in the church but afraid to yield my will to God because I didn't want to get hurt again. How would I know for sure that God was going to keep me safe, protect me? For the years that followed, this was my struggle. In 2019 my life took a turn, and thus began a new journey that led me into a very dry and difficult season. It became what I would define as my crushing season. Looking back, I realize that God was beginning to dig deep into my character.

Though the season was hard, in it, my character was being developed, and my prayer time became more and more intimate. My love grew for Him. As it grew, the more I became yielded to Him dealing with the things in me that had to go. I began to desire more and more to make God happy or to please Him. But to make God happy, I had to trust Him; I had to have faith in Him. So, He loved me right back into the place where I had to face a very deep-rooted issue—trusting Him even when I don't feel the keyword "feel" safe and protected. Thus began the next level of this journey.

But without faith, it is impossible to please him: for he that cometh to God must believe that he is, and that he is a rewarder of them that diligently seek him. Hebrews 11:6

So, as I stated earlier, during a writing session to prepare for this book, I had a revelation as well as deliverance that began to take place. It concerned a deep-rooted issue that stemmed from the departure of my dad. This is where we are on this journey to the Father. As I began to share my reason for struggling with trust, I began to consider how I felt at the moment while sharing. I was suddenly reminded of how I felt as a child before my mom was saved. Even though my mom and grandparents were in the picture, I didn't have that feeling I get now with my dad, who is now in my life. It's that great feeling that I can run to my dad, and he'll protect me.

Now that I have it, I know what was missing, and it immediately opened my eyes to my Father God. That day every hurt, every feeling of loneliness, and every reason why I felt I couldn't trust God dissipated. At that moment, and as I reflected on my life, I saw the God that I prayed to as my God and my Father God. God said in His Word that He would never leave me nor forsake me (Hebrews 13:5). He was there all the time. I was also reminded of how God kept and provided for me even in my worst state. David said in Psalms 139:8, if I ascend to heaven, God, You are there. If I make my bed in hell, God, You are there. No matter where I went, God was there, and He protected me. From that day forward, God was not only my God but my Father God. He's my Protector, the one I can run to for everything, cry out to and know that He hears me and will answer. I'm safe in my Father (Psalms 91).

This breakthrough has taken my prayer life to an even more intimate place. I literally speak to the Father about everything, and I mean EVERYTHING. The good, the bad, and the ugly. Why? Because He is and will always be there for me, He is MY FATHER.

Father God, in the Mighty Name of Jesus, I thank you for being my Father; I thank you for loving me and never leaving me. You are such an amazing Father; no matter where I've gone, no matter what I've done, you continue to be there to pull me through. Now, Father, I want to be there for You. Show me how to please you. Continue to teach me Your ways that I won't sin against You. Your love for me is so great. It's unfathomable. Father, I ask that all who read this come to know You as Father God, the One True Living God. I pray that they come to know You as their Everything. Most of all, I pray that they know Jesus as their Lord and Savior and that they have asked and received your precious gift, my dear friend, the Holy Spirit. May their lives never be the same, and may mine never be the same either. Just because of You! I Love You, Lord God, My Father God!

Monique Baker

Monique Baker, by trade, works as an Administrator, but she is, most importantly, a child of the Most High God! She loves God and His people. Monique has served as a worship leader and youth leader. She's currently the host of a weekly prayer call via Clubhouse for youth, parents, and guardians. She is the owner of a virtual administrative company and the mother of two young men who love the Lord. Her desire is to be a vessel that God can use to impact the lives of many, especially youth and families, by lifting up and introducing Jesus as the One who loves them in an incredible way!

Made in United States
Orlando, FL
16 August 2023

36121108R00065